# LaughTer

## THE BEST MEDICINE®

"Do you want a salary or benefits?"

 Gift For:

· · · · · · · · · · · · · · · · · · · · · · · · · · · ·

ƒrom:

· · · · · · · · · · · · · · · · · · · · · · · · · · · ·

Laughter the Best Medicine®
Copyright © The Reader's Digest Association, Inc.

This edition published under license from Reader's Digest, exclusively for Hallmark Cards, Inc.

Published by Hallmark Books, a division of Hallmark Cards, Inc., Kansas City, MO 64141

Visit us on the Web at Hallmark.com.

Editor: Emily Osborn
Art Director: Kevin Swanson
Designer and Production Artist: Dan Horton

Art Credits: Elwood Smith front cover, AM Alberts 9, 151, Charles Almon 103, 134, 147, Mark Anderson 56, Aaron Bacall 95, Ian Baker 77, Tim Bolton 63, Marty Bucella 25, 88, 100, John Caldwell 26, 49, 159, Scott Calvert 14, Dave Carpenter 113, Ken Catalino 110, Roy Delgado 34, 37, 55, 92, 96, 137, 138, Randy Glasbergen 116, Jeff Lok 21, Mike Lynch 31, 45, 64, 107, 148, Patricia Madigan 99, Scott Arthur Masear 22, 74, 119, Peter Mueller 52, Dan Reynolds 18, 59, 70, 73, 81, 120, 152, 156, Norm Rockwell 123, Harley Schwadron 4, 10, Mike Shapiro 87, 155, Vahan Shirvanian 42, 126, 141, Steve Smeltzer 38, 41, 131, Thomas Bros. 67, 104, Carla Ventresca 144, Kim Warp 84

ISBN: 978-1-59530-272-4

BOK3099

Printed and bound in China

# CONTeNTS

# tHis

## IS THE

# Life

**D**uring a visit to the ladies' room, my friend Addy heard the woman in the next stall suddenly ask, "So how are you?"

Startled, Addy replied tentatively, "Fine."

The woman continued, "So what's new?"

Still confused, Addy said, "Not much. What's new with you?"

It was then that the woman snapped, "Do you mind? I'm on the phone."

– Marion Sparer

"I've figured out how to send e-mails and faxes,
take photos, play games and film videos,
but what I'd really like to do is make a phone call."

"I want to try something, Caruthers—
come at me like you're asking for a raise."

I dialed a wrong number and got the following recording: "I am not available right now, but I thank you for caring enough to call. I am making some changes in my life. Please leave a message after the beep. If I do not return your call, you are one of the changes."

– Antonio Curtis

My mother, a master of guilt trips, showed me a photo of herself waiting by a phone that never rings.

"Mom, I call all the time," I said. "If you had an answering machine, you'd know." Soon after, my brother installed one for her.

When I called the next time, I got her machine: "If you are a salesperson, press one. If you're a friend, press two. If you're my daughter who never calls, press 911 because the shock will probably give me a heart attack."

– Susan Starace Balducci

It is so rare to be offered a meal on airlines these days that I was surprised to hear the flight attendant ask the man sitting in front of me, "Would you like dinner?"

"What are my choices?" he responded.

"Yes or no," she said.

– Kervyn Dimney

I recently bought a new car that had a faulty light. When, after five visits to the dealer's shop, they were unable to fix it, I tried to get it replaced by threatening to use my state's lemon laws. My calls and letters to the dealer got me nowhere.

I went to a florist, ordered a fruit basket filled with lemons and sent it to the dealer with this poem:

"When I drive my lemon, I'll be thinking of you. Pretty soon, my attorney will, too."

A short time later the dealer called and asked what color I'd like my new car to be.

– John T. Carroll

I couldn't decide whether to go to Salt Lake City or Denver for vacation, so I called the airlines to get prices. "Airfare to Denver is $300," the cheery salesperson replied.

"And what about Salt Lake City?"

"We have a really great rate to Salt Lake—$99," she said. "But there is a stopover."

"Where?"

"In Denver," she said.

— Chris Lewis

My wife was in her gynecologist's busy waiting room when a cell phone rang. A woman answered it, and for the next few minutes, she explained to her caller in intimate detail her symptoms and what she suspected might be wrong.

Suddenly the conversation shifted, and the woman said, "Him? That's over." Then she added, "Can we talk about this later? It's rather personal, and I'm in a room full of people."

— Alan Roberts

**P**ulling into my service station 45 minutes late one morning, I shouted to the customers, "I'll turn the pumps on right away!" What I didn't know was that the night crew had left them on all night. By the time I got to the office, most of the cars had filled up and driven off. Only one customer stayed to pay. My heart sank. Then the customer pulled a wad of cash from his pocket and handed it to me.

"We kept passing the money to the last guy," he said. "We figured you'd get here sooner or later."

— Jim Novak

**L**ate one night I stopped at one of those 24-hour gas station mini-marts to get myself a fresh brewed cup of coffee. When I picked up the pot, I could not help noticing that the brew was as black as asphalt and just about as thick. "How old is the coffee you have here?" I asked the woman who was standing behind the store counter.

She shrugged. "I don't know. I've only been working here two weeks."

— Peter Culver

**M**y sister Darlene has the courage—but not always the skills—to tackle any home-repair project. For example, in her garage are pieces of a lawn mower she once tried to fix. So I wasn't surprised the day my other sister, Jesse, and I found Darlene attacking her vacuum cleaner with a screwdriver.

"I can't get this thing to cooperate," she explained.

"Why don't you drag it out to the garage and show it the lawn mower?" Jesse suggested.

— Judee Norton

**M**y wife and I get along just great—except she's a back-seat driver second to none. On my way home from work one day, my cell phone rang as I merged onto a freeway bypass. It was my wife. By chance, she had entered the bypass right behind me.

"Honey," she said, "your turn signal is still on. And put your lights on—it's starting to rain."

— Wayne Ray Hairston

To keep their active two-year-old from roaming onto the busy street in front of their home, my sister and brother-in-law decided to put a gate across the driveway. After working over two weekends on the project, Robert was ready to attach the lock to complete the job. He was working on the yard side of the gate, with his daughter nearby, when he dropped the screwdriver he was using and it rolled under the gate, out of his reach.

"I'll get it, Daddy," Lauren called, nimbly crawling under the newly erected barrier.

— Janice DeCoste

My 50-something friend Nancy and I decided to introduce her mother to the magic of the Internet. Our first move was to access the popular "Ask Jeeves" site, and we told her it could answer any question she had.

Nancy's mother was very skeptical until Nancy said, "It's true, Mom. Think of something to ask it."

As I sat with fingers poised over the keyboard, Nancy's mother thought a minute, then responded, "How is Aunt Helen feeling?"

— Catherine Burns

**S**ign above the scale in a Mission Hills, Calif., doctor's office: "Pretend it's your I.Q."

– Lynn Miclea

**T**he key to success? Work hard, stay focused and marry a Kennedy.

– Arnold Schwarzenegger

**B**eing the office supervisor, I had to have a word with a new employee who never arrived at work on time. I explained that her tardiness was unacceptable and that other employees had noticed that she was walking in late every day. After listening to my complaints, she agreed that this was a problem and even offered a solution.

"Is there another door I could use?"

– Barbara Davies

**D**uring a shopping trip to a department store, I was looking around for a salesperson so I could pay for my purchase. Finally I ran into a woman wearing the store's ID tag. "Excuse me," I said. "I'm trying to locate a cashier."

"I can't help you," she briskly replied, barely slowing down. "I work in customer service." And she walked away.

– Serena Heartz

"That sounds expensive. Is there any way
you could ship it without handling it?"

**B**aseball, it is said, is only a game. True. And the Grand Canyon is only a hole in Arizona.

– George F. Will in *Fast Company*

**M**y early choice in life was either to be a piano player in a whorehouse or a politician. And to tell the truth, there's hardly any difference.

– Harry S. Truman

**I** looked up the word *politics* in the dictionary. It's actually a combination of two words: *poli*, which means many, and *tics*, which means bloodsuckers.

– Jay Leno on *"The Tonight Show"*

I was working as a short-order cook at two restaurants in the same neighborhood. On a Saturday night, I was finishing up the dinner shift at one restaurant and hurrying to report to work at the second place. But I was delayed because one table kept sending back an order of hash browns, insisting they were too cold. I replaced them several times, but still the customers were dissatisfied.

When I was able to leave, I raced out the door and arrived at my second job. A server immediately handed me my first order. "Make sure these hash browns are hot," she said, "because these people just left a restaurant down the street that kept serving them cold ones."

– Bill Bergquist

"I wrote assembly instructions for children's toys.
What did you do?"

"We're considering outsourcing your job. Could you explain to this guy in
Guatemala whatever it is you do around here?"

**E**veryone at the company I worked for dressed up for Halloween. One fellow's costume stumped us. He simply wore slacks and a white T-shirt with a large 98.6 printed across the front in glitter. When someone finally asked what he was supposed to be, he replied, "I'm a temp."

– Brian Davis


**B**ad weather meant I was stuck overnight at O'Hare airport in Chicago. Along with hotel accommodations, the airline issued each passenger a $10 meal ticket, or "chit." That evening after dinner I presented my meal ticket to the cashier.

"Is this chit worth $10?" I asked.

Looking up nervously, the cashier responded, "I'm sorry, sir. Was the meal that bad?"

– Harry Andrews

**W**hen employees of the restaurant where I work attended a fire-safety seminar, we watched a fire official demonstrate the proper way to operate an extinguisher. "Pull the pin like a hand grenade," he explained, "then depress the trigger to release the foam."

Later, an employee was selected to extinguish a controlled fire in the parking lot. In her nervousness, she forgot to pull the pin.

Our instructor hinted, "Like a hand grenade, remember?"

In a burst of confidence, she pulled the pin—and hurled the extinguisher at the blaze.

— Becki Harris

**I** got stuck in a traffic jam while commuting into Los Angeles one day. The woman in the SUV in front of me took full advantage of the slowdown. She whipped out her eyebrow pencil, lip gloss and a mirror, applying the finishing touches on her face in the ten minutes it took us to creep through the Cahuenga Pass.

Finally, the traffic broke up and as she zoomed away, I caught a glimpse of her vehicle's license plate: NTRL BTY.

— Chris Durmick

**A**s an obstetrician, I sometimes see unusual tattoos when working in labor and delivery. One patient had some type of fish tattoo on her abdomen. "That sure is a pretty whale," I commented.

With a smile she replied, "It used to be a dolphin."

– Ron Norris

**I**'m an attendant in a Laundromat. A woman came in, sat near my counter and chain-smoked cigarette after cigarette. The smoke was bothering me, so I turned on a fan. "Could you please point that thing in another direction?" she asked. "I'm just getting over pneumonia and the last thing I need is a breeze blowing on me."

– Holly Snapp

**W**hen my daughter was preparing for her school's "career week," a time when career options are discussed and often led by representatives of different professions, we talked about my job as an airline customer-services representative. I mentioned that one of my responsibilities was to load passengers' luggage at the check-in counter. I later found out to my dismay that my daughter had listed my occupation as "Bag Lady."

– Vicki Freeman

Touring Ireland's countryside with a group of travel writers, we passed an immaculate cemetery with hundreds of beautiful headstones set in a field of emerald green grass. Everyone reached for their cameras when the tour guide said the inventor of the crossword puzzle was buried there. He pointed out the location, "Three down and four across."

— Steve Bauer

Some of my co-workers and I decided to remove the small, wooden suggestion box from our office because it had received so few entries. We stuck the box on top of a seven-foot-high metal storage cabinet and then promptly forgot about it. Months later, when the box was moved during remodeling, we found a single slip of paper inside. The suggestion read, "Lower the box!"

— Frank J. Monaco

"Ah, the arbitration team is here."

# kidspeak

"Can you hear me now?"

**B**ecause it was my brother's birthday, our mom wanted to do something special. She called his fraternity house and said she wanted to bring a cake. The young man who took the call was very excited. "Hey, Mrs. Schaeffer," he said, "that would be great!"

The next day she drove to the fraternity and rang the doorbell. The same boy answered the door. When he saw the cake, his face fell. "Oh," he said, clearly disappointed. "I thought you said 'keg.' "

– Mary Schaeffer

**D**riving with my two young boys to a funeral, I tried to prepare them by talking about burial and what we believe happens after death. The boys behaved well during the service. But at the grave site I discovered my explanations weren't as thorough as I'd thought.

In a loud voice, my four-year-old asked, "Mom, what's in the box?"

– Ginny Richards

**W**hile waiting in line for the Tilt-A-Whirl, I over-heard my two nephews arguing. "Aunt Staci's going with me!" insisted Yoni. "No," said his brother, "She's going with me!"

Flattered at being so popular, I promised Yoni, "You and I can go on the merry-go-round."

"But I want you on this ride," he protested.

"Why?"

"Because the more weight, the faster it goes."

— Staci Margulis

**M**y 12-year-old daughter asked me, "Mom, do you have a baby picture of yourself? I need it for a school project." I gave her one without thinking to ask what the project was.

A few days later I was in her classroom for a par-ent-teacher meeting when I noticed my face pinned to a mural the students had created. The title of their project was "The oldest thing in my house."

— Aimee Kent

"Bobby has a Global Positioning System
on his scooter. Can I?"

"I've discovered that I'm homework intolerant."

**A** perfect parent is a person with excellent child-rearing theories and no actual children.

– Dave Barry

**T**here's no such thing as fun for the whole family.

– Jerry Seinfeld

**J**ust be good and kind to your children. Not only are they the future of the world, they're the ones who can sign you into the home.

– Dennis Miller

**D**uring our computer class, the teacher chastised one boy for talking to the girl sitting next to him.

"I was just asking her a question," the boy said.

"If you have a question, ask me," the teacher tersely replied.

"Okay," he answered. "Do you want to go out with me Friday night?"

– Tracy Maxwell

**O**ne night about 10 p.m., I answered the phone and heard, "Dad, we want to stay out late. Is that okay?"

"Sure," I answered, "as long as you called."

When I hung up, my wife asked who was on the phone. "One of the boys," I replied. "I gave them permission to stay out late."

"Not our boys," she said. "They're both downstairs in the basement."

– Lawrence M. Weisberg

"But I have learned the value of a dollar.
That's why I'm asking you for ten."

"It's a painting. There is no sound."

**M**y sister was busy getting ready to host our entire family for Easter. On her to-do list was a hair appointment for her daughter. "So, Katie," said the stylist as the little girl got up in the chair, "who's coming to your house this weekend with big ears and floppy feet?"

Katie replied, "I think it's my Uncle Brian."

– Marsha Eckerman

**A** friend of mine has an adopted son who, at six-foot-one, loves to play basketball. The boy was applying to basketball camp, and a section of the application called for him to write a brief essay about himself. My friend got a lump in his throat as he read his son's words: "Most of all I am thankful that I am adopted. . ."

Then my friend got a cold dose of reality as he continued: "because my dad is so short."

– Ralph G. Lockerbie

**R**ecently I was grading history tests for my fourth-graders. I'd included an extra-credit question: "List up to five good facts about Abraham Lincoln."

One of my D students surprised me with this one: "After the war ended, Lincoln took his wife to a show."

– Sharon Clanton

**D**on't ever pay a surprise visit to a child in college. You might be the one getting the surprise. I learned this the hard way when I swung by my son's campus during a business trip. Locating what I thought was his fraternity house, I rang the doorbell. "Yeah?" a voice called from inside.

"Does Dylan Houseman live here?"

"Yup," the voice answered. "Leave him on the front porch. We'll drag him in later."

– Jericho Houseman

"I've got to take this call."

**S**etting a good example for your children does nothing but increase their embarrassment.

– Doug Larson, United Feature Syndicate

**N**o matter how old a mother is, she watches her middle-aged children for signs of improvement.

– Florida Scott-Maxwell, *The Measure of My Days* (Knopf)

**I**f pregnancy were a book, they would cut the last two chapters.

– Nora Ephron, *Heartburn* (Knopf)

**L**ike all parents, my husband and I just do the best we can, and hold our breath and hope we've set aside enough money for our kids' therapy.

– Michelle Pfeiffer

**W**hen it comes to raising children, I believe in give and take.

I give orders and they take 'em.

– Bernie Mac in *People*

**Y**ou know your kids are growing up when they stop asking you where they came from and refuse to tell you where they're going.

– P.J. O'Rourke in *First for Women*

**V**isiting his parents' retirement village in Florida, my middle-aged friend, Tim, went for a swim in the community pool while his elderly father took a walk. Tim struck up a conversation with the only other person in the pool, a five-year-old boy. After a while, Tim's father returned from his walk and called out, "I'm ready to leave."

Tim then turned to his new friend and announced that he had to leave because his father was calling. Astonished, the wide-eyed little boy cried, "You're a kid?"

– Janice Palko

**O**ne night our local newscaster was reading about an allegation that two Sesame Street characters, Bert and Ernie, were gay. The show's producer refuted this, pointing out that they were only puppets, not humans. They argued a lot and then made up to show children how to resolve conflicts and stay friends.

While watching this report, my wife, Donna, noticed that our seven-year-old daughter was also listening. As Donna struggled to come up with an explanation for the term "gay," our crestfallen daughter said in dismay, "They're puppets?"

– Bill Doering

"Go ask your mother."

**O**n our way to my parents' house for dinner one evening, I glanced over at my 15-year-old daughter. "Isn't that skirt a bit short?" I asked. She rolled her eyes at my comment and gave me one of those "Oh, Mom" looks.

When we arrived at my folks' place, my mother greeted us at the door, hugged my daughter, then turned to me and said, "Elizabeth! Don't you think that blouse is awfully low-cut?"

– Elizabeth Scott

**M**y cooking has always been the target of family jokes. One evening, as I prepared dinner a bit too quickly, the kitchen filled with smoke and the smoke detector went off. Although both of my children had received fire-safety training at school, they did not respond to the alarm. Annoyed, I stormed through the house in search of them. I found them in the bathroom, washing their hands.

Over the loud buzzing of the smoke alarm, I asked them to identify the sound.

"It's the smoke detector," they replied in unison.

"Do you know what that sound means?" I demanded.

"Sure," my oldest replied. "Dinner's ready."

– Debi Christensen

One of my fourth graders asked my teacher's assistant, "How old are you, Mrs. Glass?"

"You should never ask an adult's age," I broke in.

"That's okay," Harriett said smiling. "I'm fifty."

"Wow, you don't look that old," the boy said. I was breathing a sigh of relief when another child chimed in, "Parts of her do."

— Katherine Norgard

My father and I belong to the religion of Sikhism. We both wear the traditional turban and often encounter strange comments and questions. Once, in a restaurant, a child stared with amazement at my father. She finally got the courage to ask, "Are you a genie?"

Her mother, caught off guard, turned red in the face and apologized for the remark. But my dad took no offense and decided to humor the child.

He replied, "Why, yes I am. I can grant you three wishes."

The child's mother blurted out, "Really?"

— Manvir Kalsi

"It's hard to believe that in just a few weeks, I'll be refusing to eat it."

**A**s my five-year-old son and I were heading to McDonald's one day, we passed a car accident. Usually when we see something terrible like that, we say a prayer for whoever might be hurt, so I pointed and said to my son, "We should pray."

From the back seat I heard his earnest voice: "Dear God, please don't let those cars block the entrance to McDonald's."

— Sherri Leard

**F**or years I had been telling my friend Pete that he ate too much fast food, but he always denied it. One day he admitted I was right.

"What changed your mind?"

"My grandson. When my daughter told him I was coming to visit, he asked, 'Grandpa from Florida, or Grandpa from Pizza Hut?' "

— Steve Frank

**F**ootball players at the high school where I worked were stealing the practice jerseys, so the coach ordered a set with "Property of Central High School" emblazoned on them. When the thefts continued, he ordered a new batch that had the imprint "Stolen From Central High School." But the jerseys still kept disappearing.

The larceny finally stopped after he changed the wording to "Central High School 4th String."

— Hal Olsen

**M**y husband, a big-time sports fan, was watching a football game with our grandchildren. He had just turned 75 and was feeling a little wistful. "You know," he said to our grandson, Nick, "it's not easy getting old. I guess I'm in the fourth quarter now."

"Don't worry, Grandpa," Nick said cheerily. "Maybe you'll go into overtime."

— Evelyn Bredleau

"Do you win every time?"

"I remind you that my client is nice until proven naughty."

had finished my Christmas shopping early and had wrapped all the presents. Having two curious children, I had to find a suitable hiding place. I chose an ideal spot— the furnace room. I stacked the presents and covered them with a blanket, positive they'd remain undiscovered.

When I went to get the gifts to put them under the tree, I lifted the blanket and there, stacked neatly on top of my gifts, were presents addressed to "Mom and Dad, From the Kids."

– Loralie Long

I fear that one day I'll meet God, he'll sneeze, and I won't know what to say."

— Ronnie Shakes, submitted by Sharon Kansas

# OPEN MOUTH, INSERT FOOT

**D**uring our church service one Sunday, a parishioner was speaking about an emotionally charged topic and had trouble controlling her tears. Finishing her remarks, she told the congregation, "I apologize for crying so much. I'm usually not such a big boob."

The bishop rose to close the session and remarked, "That's okay. We like big boobs."

– L.S.

**O**n vacation in Hawaii, my step-mom, Sandy, called a café to make reservations for 7 p.m. Checking her book, the cheery young hostess said, "I'm sorry, all we have is 6:45. Would you like that?"

"That's fine," Sandy said.

"Okay," the woman confirmed. Then she added, "Just be advised you may have to wait 15 minutes for your table."

– Kelly Finnegan

"It says, 'Separate two eggs.' Is that far enough?"

**M**y husband decided life would be easier if he wired a new light switch in the master bedroom to save us from fumbling in the dark for the lamp. He cut through the drywall and found a stash of bottles and small boxes inside the wall. "Honey!" he called excitedly. "Come see what I found!"

I ran in and quickly realized that his next task would be to fix the hole that now led into the back of our medicine cabinet.

—Nola Pirart

**M**y mother, a meticulous housekeeper, often lectured my father about tracking dirt into the house. One day he came in to find her furiously scrubbing away at a spot on the floor and launching into a lecture. "I don't know what you've brought in," she said, "but I can't seem to get this out."

He studied the situation for a moment and, without a word, moved a figurine on the windowsill where the sun was streaming in. The spot immediately disappeared.

— Michele Donnelly

**D**uring weekly visits to my allergist, I've noticed a lot of inattentive parents with ill-behaved children in the waiting room. So I was impressed one day to see a mother with her little boy, helping him sound out the words on a sign.

Finally he mastered it and his mother cheered, "That's great! Now sit there. I'll be back in 15 minutes."

What did the sign say? "Children must not be left unattended."

— Darlene Hovel

**W**hile rummaging through her attic, my friend Kathryn found an old shotgun. Unsure about how to dispose of it, she called her parents. "Take it to the police station," her mother suggested.

My friend was about to hang up when her mother added, "And Kathryn?"

"Yes, Mom?"

"Call first."

— Karen Whedon

The first day at my new health club I asked the girl at the front desk, "I like to exercise after work. What are your hours?"

"Our club is open 24/7," she told me excitedly, "Monday through Saturday."

– Apryl Cavender

Our pastor was winding down. In the back of the church, the fellowship committee stood to go to the church hall and prepare snacks for the congregation. Seeing them get up, Pastor Michel singled them out for praise.

"Before they all slip out," he urged, "let's give these ladies a big hand in the rear."

– Gordon Moore

New to the United States, I was eager to meet people. So one day I struck up a conversation with the only other woman in the gym. Pointing to two men playing racquetball in a nearby court, I said to her, "There's my husband." Then I added, "The thin one—not the fat one."

After a slightly uncomfortable silence she replied, "And that's my husband—the fat one."

– Nitya Ramakrishnan

The road by my house was in bad condition after a rough winter. Every day I dodged potholes on the way to work. So I was relieved to see a construction crew working on the road one morning.

Later, on my way home, I noticed no improvement. But where the construction crew had been working stood a new, bright-yellow sign with the words "Rough Road."

– Sarah Kraybill Lind

Over the years, my husband and I have usually managed to decode the cute but confusing gender signs they sometimes put on restroom doors in restaurants (Buoys & Gulls, Laddies & Lassies, etc.), but every so often we get stumped. Recently my husband, Dave, wandered off in search of the men's room and found himself confronted by two marked doors. One was labeled "Bronco" and the other was designated "Cactus."

Completely baffled, he stopped a restaurant employee passing by. "Excuse me, I need to use the restroom," Dave said. Gesturing toward the doors, he asked, "Which one should I use?"

"Actually, we would prefer you to go there," the employee said, pointing to a door down the hall marked "Men." "Bronco and Cactus are private dining rooms."

– Sherrie Lee

"Of course, it's nothing serious, honey...
just a flooded engine."

**A**t 82 years old, my husband applied for his first passport. He was told he would need a birth certificate, but his birth had never been officially registered. When he explained his dilemma to the passport agent, the response was less than helpful.

"In lieu of a birth certificate," the agent said, "you can bring a notarized affidavit from the doctor who delivered you."

– Elgarda Ashliman

**M**y friend Ann and I were eating at a Chinese restaurant. When an elderly waiter set chopsticks at our places, Ann made a point of reaching into her purse and pulling out her own pair. "As an environmentalist," she declared, "I do not approve of destroying bamboo forests for throwaway utensils."

The waiter inspected her chopsticks. "Very beautiful," he said politely. "Ivory."

– Erica Christensen

Thanks to my daughter, I have become thoroughly sensitized to environmental issues. Recently I purchased a greeting card, and when the cashier started to place it in a plastic bag, I remembered my daughter's repeated warnings and immediately declined its use.

"I'll be mailing that quickly," I told the clerk. "You can take the bag back."

"Okay. Have a good day," she said with a smile. Then I watched as she scrunched the bag into a ball and tossed it into the garbage.

— Arlene Kusher

After shopping for weeks, I finally found the car of my dreams. It was only two years old and in beautiful condition. The salesman asked if I would like to take it for a test drive. We had traveled no more than two miles when the car broke down. The salesman called for a tow truck.

When it arrived, we climbed into the front seat. While the driver was hooking up the car, the salesman turned to me with a smile and said, "Well, now, what is it going to take to put you behind the wheel of that beauty today?"

— Jan Baird

The college football player knew his way around the locker room better than he did the library. So when my husband's co-worker saw the gridiron star roaming the stacks looking confused, she asked how she could help. "I have to read a play by Shakespeare," he said.

"Which one?" she asked.

He scanned the shelves and answered, "William."

— Sandra J. Yarbrough

I frequently receive calls from pollsters asking me to participate in telephone surveys. One woman began with a barrage of questions.

"Wait a moment," I interrupted. "Who are you and whom do you represent?"

She told me and immediately continued asking questions.

"What's the purpose of this survey?" I asked.

"Sir," she replied irritably, "I don't have time to answer your questions." Then she hung up.

— Henry Sheppard

"Damn it, Peterson, you've got
to try and fit in!"

"There's nothing wrong with your eyesight.
You're wearing your seat belt too high!"

**F**rustrated at always being corrected by her husband, my aunt decided the next time it happened she would have a comeback. That moment finally arrived, and she was ready. "You know," she challenged, "even a broken clock is right once a day." My uncle looked at her and replied, "Twice."

– Cindy Cooksey

**W**hen I was in the sixth grade, I lost the sight in my right eye during a playground mishap. Fortunately, the accident had little effect on my life. When I reached my 40s, however, I needed to get glasses.

At the optometrist's office, the doctor's young assistant pointed to an eye chart. "Cover your right eye and read line three," she said.

"I'm blind in my right eye," I told her. "It's a glass eye."

"Okay," she responded. "In that case, cover your left eye."

– Bill Slack

**B**efore you criticize someone, you should walk a mile in their shoes. That way, when you criticize them, you're a mile away and you have their shoes.

– Quoted in *The Sisterhood of the Traveling Pants* by Ann Brashares (Delacorte Press)


**I** was having a drink at a local restaurant with my friend Justin when he spotted an attractive woman sitting at the bar. After an hour of gathering his courage, he approached her and asked, "Would you mind if I chatted with you for a while?"

She responded by yelling at the top of her lungs, "No, I won't come over to your place tonight!"

With everyone in the restaurant staring, Justin crept back to our table, puzzled and humiliated.

A few minutes later, the woman walked over to us and apologized.

"I'm sorry if I embarrassed you," she said, "but I'm a graduate student in psychology and I'm studying human reaction to embarrassing situations."

At the top of his lungs Justin responded, "What do you mean, two hundred dollars?"

– J. Smodish

**O**n a recent vacation at a resort with my in-laws, we planned to spend an afternoon at the pool with our kids. We wanted to bring our own drinks, but were unsure of the hotel's policy.

My brother-in-law called the front desk, and assuming everyone was familiar with the brand of ice chest he had, asked if it was all right if he brought a Playmate to the pool.

After a pause the clerk asked, "Does she have her own towel?"

– Tina M. Digiovanna

**W**e purchased an old home in northern New York State from two elderly sisters. Winter was fast approaching, and I was concerned about the house's lack of insulation. "If they could live here all those years, so can we!" my husband confidently declared.

One November night the temperature plunged to below zero, and we woke up to find interior walls covered with frost. My husband called the sisters to ask how they had kept the house warm. After a brief conversation, he hung up. "For the past 30 years," he muttered, "they've gone to Florida for the winter."

– Linda Dobson

**M**y husband and I were touring our friends' new home. Mr. and Mrs. Henry Curtis had put special touches everywhere. In the bathroom my husband leaned over to me and whispered, "They even have monogrammed faucets."

– Pat Gnau

**D**ispatching her ten-year-old son to pick up a pizza, my sister handed him money and a two-dollar coupon. Later he came home with the pizza, and the coupon.

When asked to explain, he replied, "Mom, I had enough money. I didn't need the coupon."

– Margaret E. Metz

**I** have a cousin who was on a plane that had taken off and was approaching cruising altitude, when one of the flight attendants came on the public-address system. She announced that she was sorry, but the plane's restroom was out of order. The flight attendant went on to apologize to the passengers for any inconvenience.

But then she finished cheerily with: "So, as compensation, free drinks will be served."

– Manjiri V. Oak

# Aging Gracelessly

"That's strange. This suit wasn't a thong last year."

**W**hen a woman I know turned 99 years old, I went to her birthday party and took some photos. A few days later, I brought the whole batch of prints to her so she could choose her favorite.

"Good Lord," she said as she was flipping through them, "I look like I'm a hundred."

– Helen B. Marrow

**M**y friend and I were celebrating our 40th birthday the same year. As a gag gift, I gave her a CD by the band UB40.

For my birthday, she retaliated with a CD as well. The group? U2.

– Mona Turrell

**S**omeone recommended a new dentist to me. On my second visit the technician finished cleaning my teeth, and as I prepared to leave, I asked brightly, "And what is your name?"

"Patricia," she answered.

"I can remember that," I commented. "It's my sister's name."

Her reply: "That's what you said last time."

– Iris Craddock

**M**y husband was bending over to tie my three-year-old's shoes. That's when I noticed my son, Ben, staring at my husband's head.

He gently touched the slightly thinning spot of hair and said in a concerned voice, "Daddy, you have a hole in your head. Does it hurt?"

After a pause, I heard my husband's murmured reply: "Not physically."

– Laurie Gerhardstein

"I do stay in shape. This is the shape I stay in."

"We all do a lot of stupid things when we're young.
So, what'll it take to remove that 'Butterball' tattoo?"

**M**y grandfather has a knack for looking on the bright side of life. Even after receiving the terrible diagnosis that he had Alzheimer's, he was philosophical.

"There's one good thing that'll come from this," he told my father.

"What's that?" asked Dad.

"Now I can hide my own Easter eggs."

— Chris Kern

**B**ecause they had no reservations at a busy restaurant, my elderly neighbor and his wife were told there would be a 45-minute wait for a table.

"Young man, we're both 90 years old," he told the maitre d'. "We may not have 45 minutes."

They were seated immediately.

— Rita Kalish

**A**ge is nothing at all...unless you are a cheese.

– Actress Billie Burke ("Glinda, the Good Witch")

**I**t's all right letting yourself go, as long as you can let yourself back.

– Mick Jagger

**W**rinkles only go where the smiles have been.

– Jimmy Buffett, *Barefoot Children in the Rain*

**R**etirement is like a long vacation in Vegas. The goal is to enjoy it to the fullest, but not so fully that you run out of money.

– Jonathan Clements in *The Wall Street Journal*

**M**y mother always used to say, "The older you get, the better you get. Unless you're a banana."

– Betty White on *"The Golden Girls"*

"You mean the older I get, the older you get?"

**F**ans of '60s music, my 14-year-old daughter and her best friend got front-row tickets to a Peter, Paul and Mary concert. When they returned home, my daughter said, "During the show, we looked back and saw hundreds of little lights swaying to the music. At first we thought the people were holding up cigarette lighters. Then we realized that the lights were the reflections off all the eyeglasses in the audience."

– Tracy Flachsbarth

**W**hile my friend Emily was visiting her mother, they went for a walk and bumped into an old family acquaintance. "Is this your daughter?" the woman asked. "Oh, I remember her when she was this high. How old is she now?"

Without pausing, Emily's mother said, "Twenty-four." Emily, 35, nearly fainted on the spot.

After everyone had said their good-byes, Emily asked her mother why she'd told such a whopper.

"Well," she replied, "I've been lying about my age for so long, it suddenly dawned on me that I'd have to start lying about yours, too."

– Robert Lee Whitmire

**A**s a professor at Texas A&M, I taught during the day and did research at night. I would usually take a break around nine, however, calling up the strategy game Warcraft on the Internet and playing with an online team.

One night I was paired with a veteran of the game who was a master strategist. With him at the helm, our troops crushed opponent after opponent, and after six games we were undefeated. Suddenly, my fearless leader informed me his mom wanted him to go to bed.

"How old are you?" I typed.

"Twelve," he replied. "How old are you?"

Feeling my face redden, I answered, "Eight."

– Todd Sayre, Ph.D.

**K**orey, my granddaughter, came to spend a few weeks with me, and I decided to teach her how to sew. After I had gone through a lengthy demonstration of how to thread the machine, Korey stepped back and put her hands on her hips. "You mean you can do all that," she said in disbelief, "but you can't operate my Game Boy?"

– Nell Baron

"Not those! At our age, we need all the
preservatives we can get."

"It's definitely hereditary. It's called aging."

I had laryngitis and finally decided to go to the doctor. After the nurse called for me, she asked my age. "Forty-nine," I whispered.

"Don't worry," she whispered back. "I won't tell anyone."

— Lola P. Bell

**M**y four-year-old nephew, Brett, had drawn a picture for his grandmother and was anxious to show it to her. Finding the door to her bathroom unlocked, he burst inside just as she was stepping out of the shower, soaking wet and without a towel.

He looked her up and down for a moment, then stated quite matter-of-factly, "Grandma, you look better with your glasses on."

– Anonymous

**T**urning 50 two years ago, I took a lot of good-natured ribbing from family and friends. So as my wife's 50th birthday approached, I decided to get in some needling of my own. I sat her down, looked deep into her eyes, then said I had never made love to anyone who was over 50 years old.

"Oh, well, I have," she deadpanned. "It's not that great."

– Bob Moreland

"I wouldn't raise my hopes too high if I were you."

"Giving up on the diet, Lenny?"

**H**aving fought the battle of the bulge most of my life, I found the battle getting even harder as I approached middle age. One evening, after trying on slacks that were too tight, I said to my husband, "I'll be so glad when we become grandparents. After all, who cares if grandmothers are fat?"

His prompt reply: "Grandfathers."

—Iris Cavin

**O**ne of the salesclerks at a local stationery store had to be a good sport to survive her 40th birthday. Not only did she have to put up with two large banners that announced: "Cathy is 40 today!" but she also had to spend the day with other saleswomen who wore tags saying: "I'm not Cathy."

– Helen Becouvarakis

**T**o celebrate his 40th birthday, my boss, who is battling middle-age spread, bought a new convertible sports car. As a finishing touch, he put on a vanity plate with the inscription "18 Again." The wind was let out of his sails, however, when a salesman entered our office the following week.

"Hey," he called out, "who owns the car with the plate 'Iate again'?"

– Cindy Gillis

The 3 stages of man.

"No gel—I mixed Rogaine and Viagra."

I wear glasses, so I can look for things I keep losing.

– Bill Cosby, *Time Flies* (Bantam Books)

Let the wind blow through your hair while you still have some.

– Dave Weinbaum

The key to successful aging is to pay as little attention to it as possible.

– Judith Regan in *More*

**M**y father, at age 93, had only the most basic needs and very few wants. Last fall, my sister-in-law, hoping to get a little help in choosing a suitable birthday gift for him, asked, "Pa, what would you like for your birthday this year?"

"Nothing," he replied.

"But, Pa," she kidded, "that's what we gave you last year."

"Well," he answered, "I'm still using it."

– L.M. Couillard

**I** was with my husband at a baseball game in Boston's Fenway Park when I decided to go get myself a hot dog. As I stood up, my husband asked me to buy him a beer. The young clerk at the concession stand asked to see verification of age.

"You've got to be kidding," I said. "I'm almost 40 years old." He apologized, but said he had to insist. When I showed him my license, the clerk served me the beer. "That will be $4.25."

I gave him $5 and told him to keep the change. "The tip's for carding me," I said.

He put the change in the tip cup. "Thanks," he said. "Works every time."

– Angie Dewhurst

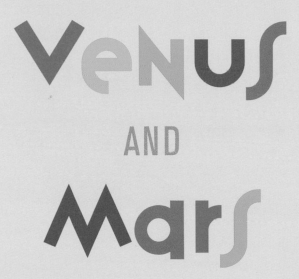

"My son's into extreme sports, my daughter's into extreme makeover, and my husband's into extreme denial."

**C**urious when I found two black-and-white negatives in a drawer, I had them made into prints. I was pleasantly surprised to see they were of a younger, slimmer me taken on one of my first dates with my husband.

When I showed him the photographs, his face lit up. "Wow! It's my old Plymouth."

– Donna Martin


**S**tanding in line at the clothing store's counter, I watched as the woman ahead of me handed the clerk her credit card. The customer waited for a long time while the saleswoman went to verify the account. When she finally returned, the clerk said, "I'm sorry, but this card is in your husband's name, and we can't accept it because the records show he is deceased."

With that, the woman turned to her spouse, who was standing next to her, and asked, "Does this mean I don't have to fix lunch for you today?"

– Marilyn Arnopol

**E**very December it was the same excruciating tradition. Our family would get up at the crack of dawn, go to a Christmas tree farm and tromp across acres of snow in search of the perfect tree. Hours later our feet would be freezing, but Mom would press on, convinced the tree of her dreams was "just up ahead."

One year I snapped. "Mom, face it. The perfect tree doesn't exist. It's like looking for a man. Just be satisfied if you can find one that isn't dead, doesn't have too many bald spots and is straight."

– Christy Martin

**D**uring my brother's wedding, my mother had managed to keep from crying—until she glanced at my grandparents. My grandmother had reached over to my grandfather's wheelchair and gently touched his hand. That was all it took to start my mother's tears flowing. After the wedding, Mom went over to my grandmother and told her how that tender gesture triggered her outburst.

"Well, I'm sorry to ruin your moment," Grandmother replied. "But I was just checking to see if he was awake."

– Mark Sample

"Romance has nothing to do with it. Dan and I
are renewing our marriage vows because
he has forgotten them."

**M**obile phones are the only subject on which men boast about who's got the smallest.

– Neil Kinnock, British politician

**T**he remarkable thing about my mother is that for 30 years she served us nothing but leftovers. The original meal has never been found.

– Calvin Trillin

**B**ehind every great man is a woman rolling her eyes.

– Jim Carrey in *"Bruce Almighty"*

**M**en want the same thing from their underwear that they want from women: a little bit of support, and a little bit of freedom.

– Jerry Seinfeld

**W**hen you're in love, it's the most glorious two-and-a-half minutes of your life.

– Richard Lewis

**H**ere's the secret to a happy marriage: Do what your wife tells you.

– Denzel Washington

"Our credit card was stolen, but I've decided not to report it. The thief is spending less than you did!"

The first time I met my wife, she was an intense aerobics instructor at my health club and I was an out-of-shape new member. After one grueling workout, I gasped, "This is really helping me get toned."

She looked me up and down. Feeling self-conscious, I added, "Big men run in my family."

She raised an eyebrow. "Apparently not enough."

– John Parker

Every year on their wedding anniversary my boss, Woody, and his wife celebrated by staying at the same resort hotel. On their 25th anniversary they booked their usual room. But when the hotel's bell captain escorted them upstairs, they were in for a big surprise.

"There must be some mistake," Woody said. "This looks like the bridal suite."

"It's okay," the bell captain reassured him. "If I put you in the ballroom, that doesn't mean you have to dance."

– Connie L. Sellers

**W**hen, by means of an at-home early pregnancy test, my wife discovered she was pregnant, she tried to get in touch with me at work. I was out, so she left a message. Later, I found a note on my desk: "E. P. T. —phone home."

– Jon Rising

**W**hile in the checkout line at my local hardware store I overheard one man say to another, "My wife has been after me to paint our shed. But I let it go for so long she got mad and did it herself."

His friend nodded. "I like women who get mad like that."

– C.V. Maynard

**W**hen a woman in my office became engaged, a colleague offered her some advice. "The first ten years are the hardest," she said.

"How long have you been married?" I asked.

"Ten years," she replied.

– Tonya Winter

"I'm going to Venus. He's going to Mars."

**M**y husband is wonderful with our baby daughter, but often turns to me for advice. Recently I was in the shower when he poked his head in to ask, "What should I feed Lily for lunch?"

"That's up to you," I replied. "There's all kinds of food. Why don't you pretend I'm not home?"

A few minutes later, my cell phone rang. I answered it to hear my husband saying, "Yeah, hi, honey. Uh. . . what should I feed Lily for lunch?"

– Julie Ball

**R**ushing to a bridge tournament, I was pulled over for going 43 in a 35 m.p.h. zone. "What'll I tell my husband?" I worried, explaining to the police officer that he was a self-described "perfect" driver.

The cop took a second look at the name and address on my license. "Did your husband go duck hunting this morning?" he asked.

Baffled, I answered, "Yes."

"I stopped him for going 47."

– Ann Alene Dunn

**M**y wife-to-be and I were at the county clerk's office for our marriage license. After recording the vital information—names, dates of birth, etc.—the clerk handed me our license and deadpanned, "No refunds, no exchanges, no warranties."

– Albert J. Campbell

**O**nce my divorce was final, I went to the local Department of Motor Vehicles and asked to have my maiden name reinstated on my driver's license. "Will there be any change of address?" the clerk inquired. "No," I replied.

"Oh, good," she said, clearly delighted. "You got the house."

– Polly Baughman

"They said he has a real fear of intimacy."

**D**riving my friend Steve and his girlfriend to the airport, we passed a billboard showing a bikini-clad beauty holding a can of beer. Steve's girlfriend glanced up at it and announced, "I suppose if I drank a six-pack of that brand, I'd look like her."

"No," Steve corrected. "If I drank a six-pack, you'd look like her."

— John D. Boyd

**M**y boyfriend and I were taking his 19-year-old niece to a weekend festival. When we arrived at her house to pick her up, she appeared in tasteful but very short shorts, and a tank top with spaghetti straps. A debate began immediately about appropriate dress. I took the girl's side, recalling that when we began dating, I dressed the same way. "Yes," said my boyfriend sternly, "and I said something about it, didn't I?"

Everyone looked at me. "Yeah," I replied. "You said, 'What's your phone number?'"

— Charnell Walls Watson

**O**ne morning I found a beautiful long-stemmed rose lying by the kitchen sink. Even though the flower was plastic, I was thinking how, after all the years we had been married, my husband could still make such a wonderful romantic gesture. Then I noticed a love note lying next to it. "Dear Sue," it read. "Don't touch the rose. I'm using the stem to unclog the drain."

– Suzan L. Wiener

**F**or years my sister's husband tried unsuccessfully to persuade her to get a hearing aid. "How much do they cost?" she asked one day after he had pitched the idea to her again.

"They're usually about $3,000," he said.

"Okay, well, if you say something worth $3,000," she replied, "I'll get one."

– Edwin A. Reinagel

**I** spent an afternoon helping my boyfriend move into a new home. In one carton, I found a crockpot with an odd-looking and very dirty metal lid. Later I ushered my boyfriend into the kitchen and asked why he hadn't mentioned this perfectly good pot.

He stared at it, then replied, "Well, after I broke the lid I never thought of replacing it with a hubcap."

– Caroline C. Jones

"Don't ask questions, Ralph. Just tell me who you'd rather look like—Sean Connery or Robert Redford."

**M**y wife, a registered nurse, once fussed over every pain or mishap that came my way. Recently, however, I got an indication that the honeymoon is over.

I was about to fix the attic fan, and as I lifted myself from the ladder into the attic, I scratched my forehead on a crossbeam. Crawling along, I picked up splinters in both hands, and I cut one hand replacing the fan belt. On the way down the ladder, I missed the last two rungs and turned my ankle.

When I limped into the kitchen, my wife took one look and said, "Are those your good pants?"

– Richard J. Schwieterman

**B**irdwatching is a passion of mine, and my wife has always been impressed by my ability to identify each species solely by its song. To help her learn a little bit about birds, I bought a novelty kitchen clock that sounds a different bird call for each hour. We were relaxing in our yard when a cardinal started singing. "What's that?" I challenged.

She listened closely. "It's three o'clock."

– Rich L. Pershey

**A** woman in my office, recently divorced after years of marriage, had signed up for a refresher CPR course. "Is it hard to learn?" someone asked.

"Not at all," she replied. "Basically you're asked to breathe life into a dummy. I don't expect to have any problem. I did that for 32 years."

– Paulette Brooks

**W**hen my wife had to rush to the hospital unexpectedly, she asked me to bring her a few items from home. One item on the list was "comfortable underwear." Worried I'd make the wrong choice, I asked, "How will I know which ones to pick?"

"Hold them up and imagine them on me," she said. "If you smile, put them back."

– Robert Kercher

**L**ove is the answer, but while you're waiting for the answer, sex raises some pretty good questions.

– Woody Allen

Instead of getting married again, I'm going to find a woman I don't like and just give her a house.

– Rod Stewart

My wife and I were comparing notes the other day. "I have a higher IQ, did better on my SATs and make more money than you," she pointed out.

"Yeah, but when you step back and look at the big picture, I'm still ahead," I said.

She looked mystified. "How do you figure?"

"I married better," I replied.

– Louis Rodolico

A friend and her husband were participating in a blood drive, and as part of the prescreening process, an elderly volunteer was asking some questions. "Have you ever paid for sex?" the woman asked my friend's husband sweetly.

Glancing wearily over at his wife, trying to calm a new baby and tend to several other children milling around her, he sighed, "Every time."

– Wendi Woolf

I was bending over to wipe up a spill on the kitchen floor when my wife walked into the room behind me. "See anything you like?" I asked suggestively.

"Yeah," she said. "You doing housework."

— Michael Shockley

One day my housework-challenged husband decided to wash his sweatshirt. Seconds after he stepped into the laundry room, he shouted to me, "What setting do I use on the washing machine?"

"It depends," I replied. "What does it say on your shirt?"

"University of Oklahoma," he yelled back.

— Jerri Boyer

At my granddaughter's wedding, the D.J. polled the guests to see who had been married the longest. Since it turned out to be my husband and me, the D.J. asked us, "What advice would you give to the newly married couple?"

I said, "The three most important words in a marriage are, 'You're probably right.' "

Everyone then looked expectantly at my husband. "She's probably right," he said.

— Barbara Hancock

"There! Now we're getting somewhere."

# pet peeves

"I could swear that box of frozen fish sticks
was here a couple of minutes ago."

**I** was at a yard sale one day and saw a box marked "Electronic cat and dog call—guaranteed to work." I looked inside and was amused to see an electric can opener.

– Bret Sohl

**M**y father's secretary was visibly distraught one morning when she arrived at the office and explained that her children's parrot had escaped from his cage and flown out an open window. Of all the dangers the tame bird would face outdoors alone, she seemed most concerned about what would happen if the bird started talking.

Confused, my father asked what the parrot could say.

"Well," she explained, "he mostly says, 'Here, kitty, kitty.' "

– Terry Walker

In good weather, my friend Mark always let his yellow-naped Amazon parrot, Nicky, sit on the balcony of his tenth-floor apartment. One morning, Nicky flew away, much to Mark's dismay. He searched and called for the bird, with no luck.

The next day, when Mark returned from work, the phone rang. "Is this Mark?" The caller asked. "You're going to think this is crazy, but there's a bird outside on my balcony saying, 'Hello, this is Mark.' Then it recites this phone number and says, 'I can't come to the phone right now, but if you will leave a message at the tone, I will call you back.'"

Nicky's cage had been kept in the same room as Mark's answering machine.

– Anne R. Neilson

"I think Mary is getting suspicious about
all the long walks."

"I'll negotiate, Stan, but I won't beg."

I was editing classified ads for a small-town newspaper when a man called to place an ad. "It should read," he said, "'*Free to good home. Golden Retriever. Will eat anything, loves children.*'"

– Ellen Young

At a workshop on dog temperament, the instructor noted that a test for a canine's disposition was for an owner to fall down and act hurt. A dog with poor temperament would try to bite the person, whereas a good dog would lick his owner's face or show concern.

Once, while eating pizza in the living room, I decided to try out this theory on my two dogs. I stood up, clutched my heart, let out a scream and collapsed on the floor.

The dogs looked at me, glanced at each other and raced to the coffee table for my pizza.

– Susan Mottice

When my daughter and I caught only one perch on our fishing trip—not enough for even a modest lunch—we decided to feed it to her two cats. She put our catch in their dish and watched as the two pampered pets sniffed at the fish but refused to eat it.

Thinking quickly, my daughter then picked up the dish, walked over to the electric can opener, ran it for a few seconds, then put the fish back down. The cats dug right in.

– Susan Ward

"You have just one more wish.
Are you sure you want *another* belly rub?"

An adorable little girl walked into my pet shop and asked, "Excuse me, do you have any rabbits here?"

"I do," I answered, and leaning down to her eye level I asked, "Did you want a white rabbit or would you rather have a soft, fuzzy black rabbit?"

She shrugged. "I don't think my python really cares."

– Cindy Patterson

Enclosed with the heartworm pills my friend received from a veterinarian was a sheet of red heart stickers to place on a calendar as a reminder to give her pet the medication. She attached these stickers to her kitchen calendar, marking the first Saturday of every month. When her husband noticed the hearts, he grinned from ear to ear, turned to his wife and asked, "Do you have something special in mind for these days?"

– Mary Louise Russo

Lost in the woods, a hiker spends two days wandering around with no food. Finally, he spots a bald eagle, hits the bird with a big rock and eats it. A park ranger stumbles on the scene and arrests the man for killing an endangered species. In court, the hiker explains that he was on the edge of starvation and had no choice.

"Considering the circumstances, I find you not guilty," says the judge. "But I have to ask—what did the eagle taste like?"

"Well, Your Honor," the hiker replies, "it tasted like a cross between a whooping crane and a spotted owl."

– Eric Fleming

A French poodle and a collie were walking down the street. The poodle turned to the collie and complained, "My life is such a mess. My owner is mean, my girlfriend is having an affair with a German shepherd and I'm as nervous as a cat."

"Why don't you go see a psychiatrist?" asked the collie.

"I can't," replied the poodle. "I'm not allowed on the couch."

– John W. Gamba

"It's my way of showing support."

**A** friend of mine is a deputy with the sheriff's department canine division. One evening, the deputy was dispatched to the scene of a possible burglary, where he discovered the back door of a building ajar. He let the dog out of his patrol car and commanded it to enter and seek.

Jumping from the back seat, the dog headed for the building. After lunging through the doorway, the dog froze and backed out. My friend was puzzled until he investigated further. Then he noticed the sign on the building: "Veterinarian's Office."

– Elizabeth Bennett

**O**ur cat, Figaro, comes home between 10 or 11 at night to eat. If he's late, I turn on the carport light and call him until he appears.

One day my daughter was explaining to a friend where we live, and her friend said, "Is that anywhere near the house where the woman stands on her steps late at night and sings opera?"

– Margaret Mathes

One afternoon I was walking on a trail with my newborn daughter, chatting to her about the scenery. When a man and his dog approached, I leaned into the baby carriage and said, "See the doggy?"

Suddenly I felt a little silly talking to my baby as if she understood me. But just as the man passed, I noticed he reached down, patted his dog and said, "See the baby?"

– Catherine Reardon

"How many times have I told you–
No coffee after September!"

"Oh, yeah, like the stripes help."

**M**y father and a friend were talking about the doors they had installed so their animals could let themselves in and out of the house. My dad asked his friend, who had two massive Great Danes, "Aren't you afraid that somebody might crawl through the dogs' door and steal something?"

"If you saw an opening that big," said his friend, "would you crawl through it?"

– Horst Jenkins

I bought my sons a pet rabbit after they promised they would take care of it. As expected, I ended up with the responsibility. Exasperated, one evening I said, "How many times do you think that rabbit would have died if I hadn't looked after it?"

"Once," my 12-year-old son replied.

— L. Barry Parsons

One day while we were doing yard work, my nine-year-old daughter found a baby snake, and I encouraged her to catch it and put it in a jar. Later she found a huge bullfrog and got another jar to put it in.

After dark I told her she would have to set them free. With the frog in one hand and the snake in the other, she started down the porch steps. Suddenly she screamed wildly, dropped both the snake and the frog, and ran into the house.

"What happened?" I asked, my heart thumping.

"Did you see that?" she replied. "That moth almost got me."

— Cassandra Dalzell

"Botox."

**Snake 1:**

Are we poisonous?

**Snake 2:**

I don't know. Why?

**Snake 1:**

I just bit my lip.

—Faith Lackey

**A**s I was walking through a variety store, I stopped at the pet department to look at some parakeets. In one cage a green bird lay on his back, one foot hooked oddly into the cage wire.

I was about to alert the saleswoman to the bird's plight when I noticed a sign taped to the cage: "No, I am not sick. No, I am not dead. No, my leg is not stuck in the cage. I just like to sleep this way."

– Joan Dezeeuw

"The first thing you have to understand is that when they throw your ball, they're not trying to get rid of you."

Sounds of crashing and banging in the middle of the night sent me and my husband out to our garage. There we spotted three raccoons eating out of the cat dish. We shooed them away and went back to bed.

Later that week we were driving home and I noticed three fat raccoons ambling down the road. "Do you think those are the same ones we chased off?" I asked.

"Hard to tell," said my husband. "They were wearing masks."

— Cherie Konvicka

Once while riding the bus to work, I noticed a man at a stop enjoying a cup of coffee. As we approached the stop, he finished drinking and set the cup on the ground. This negligence surprised me, since it seemed to be a good ceramic cup.

Days later I saw the same man again drinking his coffee at the bus stop. Once again, he placed the cup on the grass before boarding. When the bus pulled away, I looked back in time to see a dog carefully carrying the cup in his mouth as he headed for home.

– Valerie A. Huebner

If this book tickled your funny bone
or left you in stitches,
we would love to hear from you.

Please send your comments to:
Hallmark Book Feedback
P.O. Box 419034
Mail Drop 215
Kansas City, MO 64141

Or e-mail us at:
booknotes@hallmark.com